# The Writer's World: Writing Process

## Lynne Gaetz
Lionel Groulx College

## Suneeti Phadke
St. Jerome College

PEARSON

Prentice Hall

Upper Saddle River, New Jersey 07458

*Library of Congress Cataloging-in-Publication Data*

Gaetz, Lynne
The Writer's World: writing process / Lynne Gaetz, Suneeti Phadke.
p. cm.
Includes index.
ISBN 0-13-172767-2
1. English language—Paragraphs—Problems, exercises, etc.   2. English
language—Rhetoric—Problems, exercises, etc.   3. English language—Grammar—Problems,
exercises, etc.   4. English language—Textbooks for foreign speakers. 5. Report writing—
Problems, exercises, etc.   I. Phadke, Suneeti   II. Title.

PE1439.G26 2006
808'.042—dc22                                                    2005047633

**Editorial Director:** Leah Jewell
**Executive Editor:** Craig Campanella
**Acquisitions Assistant:** Joan Polk
**VP/Director, Production and Manufacturing:** Barbara Kittle
**Production Editor:** Joan E. Foley
**Production Assistant:** Marlene Gassler
**Copyeditor:** Kathryn Graehl
**Text Permissions Specialist:** Jane Scelta
**Development Editor in Chief:** Rochelle Diogenes
**Development Editor:** Veronica Tomaiuolo
**Manufacturing Manager:** Nick Sklitsis
**Prepress and Manufacturing Buyer:** Benjamin Smith
**VP/Director, Marketing:** Brandy Dawson
**Marketing Manager:** Kate Mitchell
**Marketing Assistant:** Anthony DeCosta

**Media Project Manager:** Alison Lorber
**Director, Image Resource Center:** Melinda Reo
**Manager, Image Rights and Permissions:** Zina Arabia
**Manager, Visual Research:** Beth Brenzel
**Image Permissions Coordinator:** Frances Toepfer
**Image Researcher:** Sheila Norman
**Manager, Cover Visual Research & Permissions:** Karen Sanatar
**Director, Creative Design:** Leslie Osher
**Art Director, Interior Design:** Laura Gardner
**Cover Design:** Anne DeMarinis
**Cover Art:** (front) Judith Miller Archive/Dorling Kindersley Media Library; (rear) Photodisc Green/Getty Images, Inc.; Brand X Pictures/Getty Images, Inc.; Royalty Free/CORBIS; Stockdisc Classice/Getty Images, Inc.

This book was set in 11/13 Janson by Pine Tree Composition, Inc., and was printed and bound by Courier Companies, Inc. Covers were printed by Phoenix Color Corp.

For permission to use copyrighted material, grateful acknowledgment is made to the copyright holders on page 612, which is considered an extension of this copyright page.

PEARSON EDUCATION LTD.
PEARSON EDUCATION SINGAPORE, PTE. LTD
PEARSON EDUCATION, CANADA, LTD
PEARSON EDUCATION–JAPAN
PEARSON EDUCATION AUSTRALIA PTY, LIMITED

PEARSON EDUCATION NORTH ASIA LTD
PEARSON EDUCACIÓN DE MEXICO, S.A. DE C.V.
PEARSON EDUCATION MALAYSIA, PTE. LTD
PEARSON EDUCATION, UPPER SADDLE RIVER, NJ

10  9  8  7  6  5  4  3  2

ISBN 0-13-172767-2

# Contents

## PART I — The Writing Process   2

 **CHAPTER 1   Exploring**   3

 **CHAPTER 2   Developing**   16

 **CHAPTER 3   Revising and Editing**   38

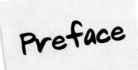

# About the Individual Volumes of *The Writer's World: Paragraphs and Essays*

Prentice Hall is proud to offer *The Writer's World: Paragraphs and Essays* in four individual volumes—all created directly from the pages of the parent text by Lynne Gaetz and Suneeti Phadke:

- *The Writer's World: Writing Process* (Part I, Chapters 1-3)
- *The Writer's World: Paragraph Patterns and the Essay* (Parts II-III, Chapters 4-15)
- *The Writer's World: Editing Handbook* (Part IV, Chapters 16-36)
- *The Writer's World: Reading Strategies and Selections* (Part V, Chapter 37)

Instructors teach writing in different ways. Developed for maximum flexibility, *The Writer's World* volumes help instructors tailor courses to their specific needs. For example, instructors who prefer using their own reading selections may choose only the first three volumes. Other instructors may want to take advantage of only thematic grammar, so they might choose only the third volume.

Other features of *The Writer's World* individual volumes include:

**Value:** Each volume sells at a price significantly less than the parent text. This value pricing allows instructors who require three or fewer volumes for the course to give students the option of purchasing only the volumes they need to fulfill course requirements.

**Page Numbers:** The page numbers remain consistent with the page numbers in the parent text. As a result, an instructor using the Annotated Instructor's Edition can easily work with an entire class regardless of which students are using individual volumes and which are using the parent text.

**Links:** The parent text contains margin references (Writing Links, Reading Links, and Grammar Links) that connect material to other parts of the book. Since students using only individual volumes will not have access to all of the linked pages, we have eliminated some links from these books.

**Resources:** *The Writer's World* has a rich collection of resources for college adopters of both the parent text and the individual volumes. Any two of the following supplements may be packaged with a volume at no additional cost:

- The Visualizing Writing CD-ROM (ISBN: 0-13-194108-9)
- The Prentice Hall Grammar Workbook, Second Edition (0-13-194771-0)
- The Prentice Hall Editing Workbook (0-13-189352-1)
- Applying English to Your Career (0-13-192115-0)
- The Prentice Hall ESL Workbook, Second Edition (0-13-194759-1)
- The Prentice Hall Writer's Journal (0-13-184900-X)
- *The New American Webster Handy College Dictionary* (0-13-045258-0)
- *The New American Roget's College Thesaurus* (0-13-045258-0)

Many more packaging options are available. For a complete listing, please contact your local Prentice Hall representative.

# About the First Edition of *The Writer's World: Writing Process*

Whether your students enroll in the course with varying skill levels, whether they are native or nonnative speakers of English, or whether they learn better through the use of visuals, *The Writer's World* can help students produce writing that is technically correct and rich in content. It is our goal for this preface to give you a deeper understanding of how we arranged the text and the key components found in *The Writer's World: Paragraphs and Essays*.

## A Research-Based Approach

From the onset of the development process, we have comprehensively researched the needs and desires of current developmental writing instructors. We met with more than 45 instructors from around the country, asking for their opinions and insights regarding (1) the challenges posed by the course, (2) the needs of today's ever-changing student population, and (3) the ideas and features we were proposing in order to provide them and you with a more effective learning and teaching tool. Prentice Hall also commissioned dozens of detailed manuscript reviews from instructors, asking them to analyze and evaluate each draft of the manuscript. These reviewers identified numerous ways in which we could refine and enhance our key features. Their invaluable feedback was incorporated throughout *The Writer's World*. The text you are seeing is truly the product of a successful partnership between the authors, publisher, and well over 100 developmental writing instructors.

## How We Organized
## *The Writer's World*

**Part I: The Writing Process** teaches students (1) how to formulate ideas (Exploring); (2) how to expand, organize, and present those ideas in a piece of writing (Developing); and (3) how to polish writing so that they convey their message as clearly as possible (Revising and Editing). The result is that writing a paragraph or an essay becomes far less daunting because students have specific steps to follow.

## How *The Writer's World* Meets Students' Diverse Needs

We created *The Writer's World* to meet your students' diverse needs. To accomplish this, we asked both the instructors in our focus groups and the reviewers at every stage not only to critique our ideas but to offer their suggestions and recommendations for features that would enhance the learning process of their students. The result has been the integration of many elements that are not found in other textbooks, including our visual program, coverage of nonnative speaker material, and strategies for addressing the varying skill levels students bring to the course.

## The Visual Program

A stimulating, full-color book, *The Writer's World* recognizes that today's world is a visual one, and it encourages students to become better communicators by responding to images. Chapter opening visuals in Part I help students to think about the chapter's key concepts in new ways. For example, in Chapter 1, 2, and 3 openers, photographs of an artist at work sets the stage for the steps of the writing process.

## Seamless Coverage for Nonnative Speakers

Instructors in our focus groups noted the growing number of nonnative/ESL speakers enrolling in the developmental writing courses. Although some of

these students have special needs relating to the writing process, many of you still have a large portion of native speakers in your courses whose more traditional needs must also be satisfied. To meet the challenge of this rapidly changing dynamic, we have carefully implemented and integrated content throughout to assist these students. *The Writer's World* does not have separate ESL boxes, ESL chapters, or tacked-on ESL appendices. Instead, information that traditionally poses challenges to nonnative speakers is woven seamlessly throughout the book. In our extensive experience teaching writing to both native and nonnative speakers of English, we have learned that both groups learn best when they are not distracted by ESL labels. With the seamless approach, nonnative speakers do not feel self-conscious and segregated, and native speakers do not tune out to detailed explanations that may also benefit them. Many of these traditional problem areas receive more coverage than you would find in other textbooks, arming the instructor with the material to effectively meet the needs of nonnative speakers.

## What Tools Can Help Students Get the Most from *The Writer's World*?

Overwhelmingly, focus group participants and reviewers asked that both a larger number and a greater diversity of exercises and activities be incorporated into a new text. In response to this feedback, we have developed and tested the following items in *The Writer's World*. These tools form the pedagogical backbone of the book, and we are confident they will help your students become better writers.

## Hints

In each chapter, **Hint** boxes highlight important writing and grammar points. Hints are useful for all students, but many will be particularly helpful for nonnative speakers.

## The Writer's Desk

Part I includes **The Writer's Desk** exercises that help students get used to practicing all stages and steps of the writing process. Students begin with prewriting and then progress to developing, organizing (using paragraph and essay plans), drafting, and finally, revising and editing to create a final draft.

## Reflect On It

Each **Reflect On It** is a chapter review exercise. Questions prompt students to recall and review what they have learned in the chapter.

## The Writer's Room

**The Writer's Room** contains writing activities that correspond to general, college, and workplace topics. Some prompts are brief to allow students to freely form ideas while others are expanded to give students more direction.

There is literally something for every student writer in this end-of-chapter feature. Students who respond well to visual cues will appreciate the photo writing exercises. Students who learn best by hearing through collaboration will appreciate the discussion and group work prompts in **The Writers' Circle** section of selected **The Writer's Rooms.**

# Acknowledgments

Many people have helped us produce *The Writer's World*. First and foremost, we would like to thank our students for inspiring us and providing us with extraordinary feedback. Their words and insights pervade this book.

We also benefited greatly from the insightful comments and suggestions from over 200 instructors across the nation, all of whom are listed in the opening pages of the Annotated Instructor's Edition. Our colleagues' feedback was invaluable and helped shape *The Writer's World* series content, focus, and organization.

We are indebted to the team of dedicated professionals at Prentice Hall who have helped make this project a reality. They have boosted our spirits and have believed in us every step of the way. Special thanks to Veronica Tomaiuolo for her magnificent job in polishing this book and to Craig Campanella for trusting our instincts and enthusiastically propelling us forward. Kate Mitchell worked tirelessly to ensure we were always meeting the needs of instructors. We owe a deep debt of gratitude to Yolanda de Rooy, whose encouraging words helped ignite this project. Joan Foley's attention to detail in the production process kept us motivated and on task and made *The Writer's World* a much better resource for both instructors and students. We would also like to thank Laura Gardner for her brilliant design, which helped keep the visual learner in all of us engaged.

Finally, we would like to dedicate this book to our husbands and children who supported us and who patiently put up with our long hours on the computer. Manu, Octavio, and Natalia continually encouraged us. We especially appreciate the help and sacrifices of Diego, Becky, Kiran, and Meghana.

# A Note to Students

Your knowledge, ideas, and opinions are important. The ability to clearly communicate those ideas is invaluable in your personal, academic, and professional life. When your writing is error-free, readers will focus on your message, and you will be able to persuade, inform, entertain, or inspire them. *The Writer's World* includes strategies that will help you improve your written communication. Quite simply, when you become a better writer, you become a better communicator. It is our greatest wish for *The Writer's World* to make you excited about writing, communicating, and learning.

Enjoy!
Lynne Gaetz and Suneeti Phadke
TheWritersWorld@hotmail.com

Lynne Gaetz and family in Mexico

Suneeti Phadke and family in Quebec, Canada

# The Writing Process

## An Overview

**T**he writing process is a series of steps that most writers follow to get from thinking about a topic to preparing the final draft. Generally, you should follow the process step by step; however, sometimes you may find that your steps overlap. For example, you might do some editing before you revise, or you might think about your main idea while you are prewriting. The important thing is to make sure that you have done all of the steps before preparing your final draft.

Before you begin the next chapters, review the steps in the writing process.

### Exploring

Step 1: Think about your topic.

Step 2: Think about your audience.

Step 3: Think about your purpose.

Step 4: Try exploring strategies.

### Developing

Step 1: Narrow your topic.

Step 2: Express your main idea.

Step 3: Develop your supporting ideas.

Step 4: Make a plan or an outline.

Step 5: Write your first draft.

### Revising and Editing

Step 1: Revise for unity.

Step 2: Revise for adequate support.

Step 3: Revise for coherence.

Step 4: Revise for style.

Step 5: Edit for technical errors.

# Exploring

## CHAPTER 1

*"Writing is an exploration. You start from nothing and learn as you go."*

—E. L. DOCTOROW
*American author (b. 1931)*

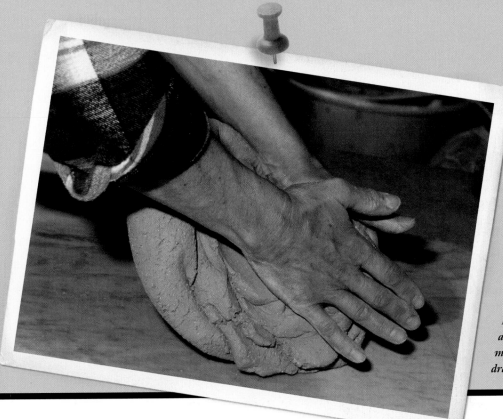

*Before placing clay on a pottery wheel, a potter takes time to consider what to make. Similarly, before developing a draft, a writer needs to explore the topic.*

## The Paragraph and the Essay

Most of the writing that we do—e-mail messages, work reports, college papers—is made up of paragraphs and essays. A **paragraph** is a series of sentences that are about one central idea. Paragraphs can stand alone or they can be part of a longer work such as an essay, a letter, or a report. An **essay** is a series of paragraphs that are about one central idea. Both the paragraph and the essay are divided into three parts.

### Characteristics of a Paragraph

- The **topic sentence** introduces the subject of the paragraph and shows the writer's attitude towards the subject.

- The **body** of the paragraph contains details that support the topic sentence.

- The paragraph ends with a **concluding sentence.**

### Characteristics of an Essay

- The **introduction** engages the reader's interest and contains the **thesis statement.**

- The **body** paragraphs each support the main idea of the essay.

- The **conclusion** reemphasizes the thesis and restates the main points of the essay. It brings the essay to a satisfactory close.

Look at the relationship between paragraphs and essays. Both examples are about real-life heroes. However, in the essay, each supporting idea is expanded into paragraph form.

**The Paragraph**                    **The Essay**

**Thesis statement:** The public should pay more attention to real-life heroes.

**Support 1:** Firefighters risk their lives to save others.

**Topic sentence:** The public should pay more attention to real-life heroes. **Support 1:** Firefighters risk their lives to save others. **Support 2:** Without police officers, there would be chaos in the streets. **Support 3:** Medical staff and researchers save lives and cure diseases. **Conclusion:** Instead of focusing on celebrities, learn about the heroes among us.

**Support 2:** Without police officers, there would be chaos in the streets.

**Support 3:** Medical staff and researchers save lives and cure diseases.

**Conclusion:** Instead of focusing on celebrities, learn about the heroes among us.

All writing begins with ideas. In the next section of this chapter, you will practice ways to explore ideas.

**ESSAY LINK**

When you plan an essay, you should follow the four exploring steps.

# What Is Exploring?

Have you ever been given a writing subject and then stared at the blank page, thinking, "I don't know what to write?" Well, it is not necessary to write a good paragraph or essay immediately. There are certain things that you can do to help you focus on your topic.

## Understand Your Assignment

As soon as you are given an assignment, make sure that you understand what your task is. Answer the following questions about the assignment:

- How many words or pages should I write?
- What is the due date for the assignment?
- Are there any special qualities my writing should include?

After you have considered your assignment, follow the four steps in the exploring stage of the writing process.

---

### EXPLORING

| | |
|---|---|
| **STEP 1** | ➤ **Think about your topic.** Determine what you will write about. |
| **STEP 2** | ➤ **Think about your audience.** Consider your intended readers and what interests them. |
| **STEP 3** | ➤ **Think about your purpose.** Ask yourself why you want to write. |
| **STEP 4** | ➤ **Try exploring strategies.** Experiment with different ways to generate ideas. |

---

# Topic

Your **topic** is what you are writing about. When an instructor gives you a topic for your writing, you can give it a personal focus. For example, if the instructor asks you to write about "travel," you can take many approaches to the topic. You might write about the dangers in travel, describe a trip that you have taken, or explain the lessons that travel has taught you. When you are given a topic, find an angle that interests you and make it your own.

When you think about the topic, ask yourself the following questions.

- What about the topic interests me?
- Do I have special knowledge about the topic?
- Does anything about the topic arouse my emotions?

# Audience

Your **audience** is your intended reader. In your personal, academic, and professional life, you will often write for a specific audience; therefore, you can keep your readers interested by adapting your tone and vocabulary to suit them. **Tone** is your general attitude or feeling toward a topic. For example, you might write in a tone that is humorous, sarcastic, serious, friendly, or casual.

When you consider your audience, ask yourself the following questions.

- Who will read my assignment—an instructor, other students, or people outside the college?
- Do my readers have a lot of knowledge about my topic?
- Will my readers expect me to write in proper, grammatically correct English?

In academic writing, your audience is generally your instructor or other students, unless your instructor specifically asks you to write for another audience such as the general public, your employer, or a family member.

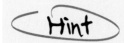

**Hint** **Instructor as the Audience**

When you write for your instructor, use standard English. In other words, try to use correct grammar, sentence structure, and vocabulary. Also, do not leave out information because you assume that your instructor is an expert in the field. Generally, when your instructor reads your work, he or she will expect you to reveal what you have learned or what you have understood about the topic.

## PRACTICE I

E-mail messages A and B are about career goals. As you read the messages, consider the differences in both the tone and the vocabulary the writer uses. Then answer the questions that follow. Circle the letter of the correct answer.

1. Who is the audience for E-mail A?
   a. A friend
   b. A family member
   c. A potential employer
   d. An instructor

2. Who is the audience for E-mail B?
   a. A friend
   b. A family member
   c. A potential employer
   d. An instructor

**E-mail A**

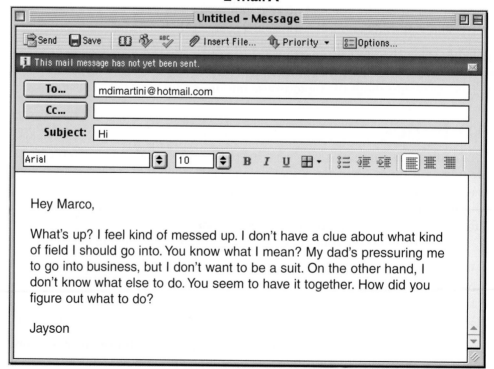

Hey Marco,

What's up? I feel kind of messed up. I don't have a clue about what kind of field I should go into. You know what I mean? My dad's pressuring me to go into business, but I don't want to be a suit. On the other hand, I don't know what else to do. You seem to have it together. How did you figure out what to do?

Jayson

**E-mail B**

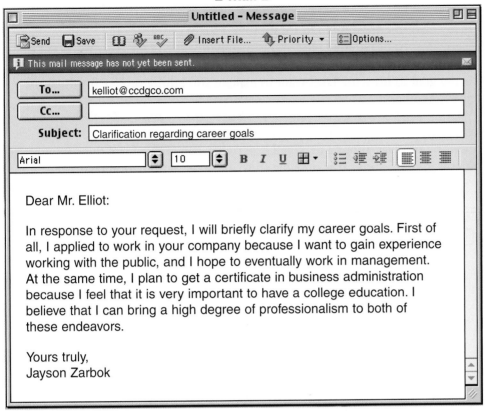

3. In a word or two, describe the tone in each e-mail.

E-mail A: _____ E-mail B: _____

4. **Language clues** are words or phrases that help you determine the audience. What language clues helped you determine the audience of E-mails A and B? The first clue in each e-mail message has been identified for you.

E-mail A: _____ E-mail B: _____

Hey Marco,                    Dear Mr. Elliot:

_____              _____

_____              _____

_____              _____

_____              _____

# Purpose

Your **purpose** is your reason for writing. Keeping your purpose in mind will help you focus your writing.

When you consider your purpose, ask yourself the following questions.

- Is my goal to **entertain?** Do I want to tell a story?
- Is my goal to **persuade?** Do I want to convince the reader that my point of view is the correct one?
- Is my goal to **inform?** Do I want to explain something or give information about a topic?

Sometimes you may have more than one purpose. For example, a narrative paragraph or essay about a personal experience can also inform the reader about something interesting. It is possible to write for a combination of reasons.

 **General and Specific Purpose**

Your **general purpose** is to entertain, to inform, or to persuade. Your **specific purpose** is your more precise reason for writing. For example, imagine that you have to write a piece about music. Your general purpose may be to inform while your specific purpose may be to explain how to become a better musician.

## PRACTICE 2

Selections 1 to 3 are about music; however, each has a different purpose, has been written for a different audience, and has been taken from a different source. To complete this practice, read each selection carefully. Then underline any language clues (words or phrases) that help you identify its source, audience, and purpose. Finally, answer the questions that follow each selection.

**EXAMPLE:**

Slang ➤     I'm totally <u>psyched</u> about learning the drums. It's taken me a while to get used to keeping up a steady beat, but I think I'm getting it. My drum teacher is
Slang, informal tone ➤ <u>cool</u>, and he's <u>pretty patient</u> with me. I try to practice, but it bugs the neighbors when I hit the cymbals.

What is the most likely source of this paragraph?

    a. web site article    b. novel    c. textbook    (d.) personal letter

What is its purpose? _To inform_

Who is the audience? _Friend or family member_

1.     Lomax also found a relationship between polyphony, where two or more melodies are sung simultaneously, and a high degree of female participation in food-getting. In societies in which women's work is responsible for at least half of the food, songs are likely to contain more than one simultaneous melody, with the higher tunes usually sung by women.

What is the most likely source of this paragraph?

    a. web site article    b. novel    c. textbook    d. personal letter

What is its purpose? _____

Who is the audience? _____

_____

2.    When dealing with club managers, it is *imperative* that you act professionally. Get all the details of a gig in advance. Doing so will eliminate any confusion or miscommunication that could result in a botched deal. It will also instantly set you apart from the legions of flaky musicians that managers must endure on a daily basis. That's a good thing.

What is the most likely source of this paragraph?

a. web site article      b. novel      c. textbook      d. personal letter

What is its purpose? _____

Who is the audience? _____

_____

3.    But there was no reason why everyone should not dance. Madame Ratignolle could not, so it was she who gaily consented to play for the others. She played very well, keeping excellent waltz time and infusing an expression into the strains which was indeed inspiring. She was keeping up her music on account of the children, she said, because she and her husband both considered it a means of brightening the home and making it attractive.

What is the most likely source of this paragraph?

a. web site article      b. novel      c. textbook      d. personal letter

What is its purpose? _____

Who is the audience? _____

_____

# Exploring Strategies

After you determine your topic, audience, and purpose, try some **exploring strategies**—also known as **prewriting strategies**—to help get your ideas flowing. The four most common strategies are *freewriting, brainstorming, questioning,* and *clustering.* It is not necessary to do all of the strategies explained in this chapter. Find the strategy that works best for you.

## Freewriting

**Freewriting** is writing for a limited period of time without stopping. The point is to record the first thoughts that come to mind. If you have no ideas, you can indicate that fact in a sentence such as "I don't know what to write." As you write, do not be concerned with your grammar or spelling. If you use a computer, let your ideas flow and do not worry about typing mistakes.

 **When to Use Exploring Strategies**

You can use exploring strategies at any stage of the writing process.

• To find a topic

• To narrow a broad topic

• To generate ideas about your topic

• To generate supporting details

**TECHNOLOGY LINK**

On a computer, try typing without looking at the screen or with the screen turned off. Don't worry about mistakes.

### SANDRA'S FREEWRITING

College student Sandra Ahumada did freewriting about work. During her freewriting, she wrote everything that came to mind.

> Work. I've only worked in a restaurant. A lot of reasons to work in a restaurant. Schedules are good for college students. Can work nights or weekends. Serving people so different from studying. You can relax your brain, go on automatic pilot. But you have to remember people's orders so it can be hard. And some customer are rude, rude, RUDE. What else . . . It is hard to juggle a job and college work. But it forces me to organize my time. What types of jobs pay a good salary? Day-care work? In some jobs, you get tips in addition to the salary. The tips can be very good. Like for hairdressers. Taxi drivers.

### PRACTICE 3

In Sandra's freewriting, underline each idea that could be expanded into a complete paragraph.

## *The Writer's Desk* Freewriting

Choose one of the following topics and do some freewriting. Remember to write without stopping.

The family              Travel              Telling lies

## Brainstorming

**Brainstorming** is like freewriting except that you create a list of ideas, and you can take the time to stop and think when you create your list. As you think about the topic, write down words or phrases that come to mind. Do not be concerned about grammar or spelling; the point is to generate ideas.

##### WADE'S BRAINSTORMING

College student Wade Vong brainstormed about city life. He made a list of ideas.

- living in a city vs. living in a town
- my favorite cities
- the bad side of city life
- reasons people move to large cities
- Los Angeles full of pollution
- reasons to live in a large city
- my impressions of Las Vegas
- reasons to get out of cities
- the physical differences between rich and poor neighborhoods
- developing the inner city to keep it vibrant

### PRACTICE 4

Underline any of Wade's ideas that could be developed into complete paragraphs.

### The Writer's Desk **Brainstorming**

Choose one of the following topics and brainstorm. Write down a
list of ideas.

Ceremonies     An issue in the news     Good or bad manners

## Questioning

Another way to generate ideas about a topic is to ask yourself a series of questions
and write responses to them. The questions can help you define and narrow your
topic. One common way to do this is to ask yourself *who, what, when, where, why,*
and *how* questions.

##### CLAYTON'S QUESTIONING

College student Clayton Rukavina used a question-and-answer format to generate
ideas about binge drinking.

| | |
|---|---|
| What is binge drinking? | having too much alcohol in a short time |
| Who binge-drinks? | students who are away from home for the first time, or insecure students |
| Why do students drink too much? | peer pressure, want to be more relaxed, don't think about consequences |
| When do students drink too much? | spring break, weekends, to celebrate legal age |
| How dangerous is binge drinking? | may get alcohol poisoning, may choke, and may drink and drive |
| Where does it happen? | dorm rooms, house parties, fraternities |
| Why is it an important topic? | can die from binge drinking or drunk driver can kill somebody else |

**PRACTICE 5**

Underline any of Clayton's ideas that could be developed into complete paragraphs.

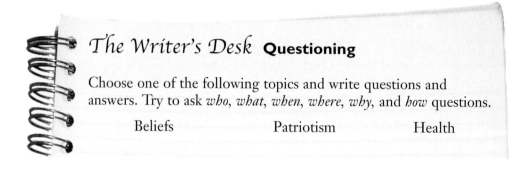

*The Writer's Desk* **Questioning**

Choose one of the following topics and write questions and answers. Try to ask *who, what, when, where, why,* and *how* questions.

| Beliefs | Patriotism | Health |

## Clustering

**Clustering** is like drawing a word map; ideas are arranged in a visual image. To begin, write your topic in the middle of the page and draw a box or a circle around it. That idea will lead to another, so write the second idea, and draw a line connecting it to your topic. Keep writing, circling, and connecting ideas until you have groups or "clusters" of them on your page.

### ADELA'S CLUSTERING

College student Adela Santana used clustering to explore ideas about crime. She identified some main topics. Then she created clusters around each topic.

**PRACTICE 6**

Look at Adela's clustering. Think of two other topics that she could add to her cluster.

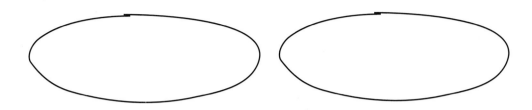

### The Writer's Desk **Clustering**

Choose one of the following topics and make a cluster on a separate sheet of paper. Begin by writing the key word in the middle of the space. Then connect related ideas.

Jobs                    College                    Relationships

# Journal and Portfolio Writing

## Keeping a Journal

You may write for work or school, but you can also practice writing for pleasure. One way to practice your writing is to keep a journal. A **journal** is a book, a computer file, or a blog (Web log) where you record your thoughts, opinions, ideas, and impressions. Journal writing gives you a chance to practice your writing without worrying about your readers and what they might think about it. It also gives you a source of material when you want to write about a topic of your choice. According to the author Anaïs Nin, "Keeping a diary is a way of making everyday life seem as exciting as fiction."

In your journal, you can write about any topic that appeals to you. Here are some topics for journal writing.

- Anything related to your personal life, such as your feelings about your career goals, personal problems and solutions, opinions about your college courses, reflections about past and future decisions, or feelings about your job
- Your reactions to controversies in the world, in your country, in your state, in your city, or in your college
- Facts that interest you
- Your reflections on the opinions and philosophies of others, including your friends or people that you read about in your courses

## Keeping a Portfolio

A **writing portfolio** is a binder or an electronic file folder where you keep samples of all of your writing. The purpose of keeping a portfolio is to have a record of your writing progress. In your portfolio, keep all drafts of your writing assignments. When you work on new assignments, review your previous work in your portfolio. Identify your main problems, and try not to repeat the same errors.

## REFLECT ON IT

Think about what you learned in this chapter. If you do not know an answer, review that topic.

1. Before you write, you should think about your topic, audience, and purpose. Explain what each one is.

   a. Topic: _____

   b. Audience: _____

   c. Purpose: _____

2. Briefly define each of the following exploring styles.

   a. Freewriting: _____

   b. Brainstorming: _____

   c. Questioning: _____

   d. Clustering: _____

 *The Writer's Room* **Topics to Explore**

## Writing Activity 1

Choose one of the following topics, or choose your own topic. Then generate ideas about the topic. You may want to try the suggested exploring strategy.

### General Topics

1. Try freewriting about a strong childhood memory. Try freewriting about your childhood.

2. Try brainstorming and list any thoughts that come to mind about anger.

3. Try clustering. First, write "Rules" in the middle of the page. Then write clusters of ideas that connect to the general topic.

4. Ask and answer some questions about cosmetic surgery.

### College and Work-Related Topics

5. Try freewriting about a comfortable place. Include any emotions or other details that come to mind.

6. Try brainstorming about study or work habits. List any ideas that come to mind.

7. To get ideas, ask and answer questions about gossip.

8. Try clustering. First, write "Cell phones" in the middle of the page. Then write clusters of ideas that relate to the general topic.

## Writing Activity 2

Look carefully at the poster. Use questioning as your exploring strategy. Ask and answer *who, what, when, where, why,* and *how* questions.

![checkmark icon] **EXPLORING CHECKLIST**

As you explore your topics, ask yourself the following questions.

☐ What is my topic? (Consider what you will write about.)

☐ Who is my audience? (Think about your intended reader.)

☐ What is my purpose? (Determine your reason for writing.)

☐ How can I explore? (You might try freewriting, brainstorming, questioning, or clustering.)

## CHAPTER 2

# Developing

*"You can only learn to be a better writer by actually writing."*

—DORIS LESSING
*British author (b. 1919)*

*After finding an idea, a potter begins to knead and shape the clay. Like a potter, a writer shapes ideas to create a solid paragraph or essay.*

## What Is Developing?

In Chapter 1, you learned how to narrow topics and how to use exploring strategies to formulate ideas. In this chapter, you will focus on the second stage of the writing process: **developing.** There are five key steps in the developing stage.

### DEVELOPING

STEP 1 → **Narrow your topic.** Focus on some aspect of the topic that interests you.

STEP 2 → **Express your main idea.** Write a topic sentence (for a paragraph) or a thesis statement (for an essay) that expresses the main idea of the piece of writing.

STEP 3 → **Develop your supporting ideas.** Find facts, examples, or anecdotes that best support your main idea.

STEP 4 → **Make a plan.** Organize your main and supporting ideas, and place your ideas in a plan or an outline.

STEP 5 → **Write your first draft.** Communicate your ideas in a single written piece.

## Reviewing Paragraph Structure

Before you practice developing your paragraphs, review the paragraph structure. A **paragraph** is a series of related sentences that develop one central idea. Because a paragraph can stand alone or be part of a longer piece of writing, it is the essential writing model. You can apply your paragraph writing skills to longer essays, letters, and reports.

A stand-alone paragraph generally has the following characteristics.

- A **topic sentence** states the topic and introduces the idea the writer will develop.
- **Body sentences** support the topic sentence.
- A **concluding sentence** ends the paragraph.

### CATHERINE'S PARAGRAPH

College student Catherine Niatum wrote the following paragraph. Read her paragraph and notice how it is structured.

> **The commercialization of traditional holidays helps our economy.** People spend a lot of money celebrating religious and popular holidays. For example, the clothing industry benefits because people spend money on new outfits. Also, toy stores and other gift shops profit when the public celebrates by giving presents to loved ones. Department stores see their sales increase when customers buy special lights, candles, and other decorations for their homes. Grocery stores and restaurants profit during holiday seasons because people prepare feasts, and companies have staff parties in restaurants and hotels. Finally, the travel industry has a financial windfall during celebrations such as Thanksgiving because people cross the nation to visit their loved ones. The next time anyone complains about the commercialization of holidays, remind the person that holiday spending is very beneficial for our economy.

◅ The topic sentence expresses the idea that Catherine develops in the paragraph.

◅ Catherine supports the paragraph with examples.

◅ The concluding sentence brings the paragraph to a satisfying close.

---

 **Paragraph Form**

When you write a paragraph, make sure that it has the following form.

- Always indent the first word of a paragraph. Move it about one inch, or five spaces, from the left-hand margin.

- Try to leave a margin of an inch to an inch and a half on each side of your paragraph.

> The legal drinking age is an ineffective deterrent to underage drinking.

# Narrow the Topic

A paragraph has one main idea. If your topic is too broad, you might find it difficult to write only one paragraph about it. When you **narrow** your topic, you make it more specific.

To narrow your topic, you can use exploring strategies such as freewriting, brainstorming, and questioning. These strategies are explained in more detail in Chapter 1, "Exploring."

Review the following examples of general and narrowed topics.

**ESSAY LINK**

An essay contains several paragraphs and can have a broader topic than a paragraph.

| General Topic | Narrowed Topic |
|---|---|
| The job interview | How to dress for a job interview |
| College | My misconceptions about college life |
| Rituals | The high school prom |

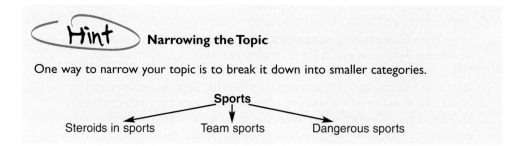

> **Hint**   **Narrowing the Topic**

One way to narrow your topic is to break it down into smaller categories.

**Sports**

Steroids in sports      Team sports      Dangerous sports

## SANDRA'S EXAMPLE OF NARROWING A TOPIC

College student Sandra Ahumada practiced narrowing a topic by thinking of ideas about work.

- types of work: paid work, housework, homework
- jobs I have done in the service industry: server, cashier
- reasons to work in a restaurant
- how to find a job
- bad jobs that I have had
- finding the right career
- dangerous jobs such as firefighter, police officer
- are online job sites useful?

## The Writer's Desk   Narrow the Topic

Topics 1 to 5 are very broad. Practice narrowing topics by writing three ideas for each one.

**EXAMPLE:** City life:   _living in a city vs. living in a small town_

_impressions of Las Vegas_

_keeping the inner cities vibrant_

1. The family: _____

   _____

   _____

2. Telling lies: _____

   _____

   _____

3. Travel: _____

   _____

   _____

4. An issue
   in the news: _____

   _____

   _____

5. Jobs: _____

   _____

   _____

After you have narrowed your topic, you can develop your topic sentence.

# The Topic Sentence

After you have narrowed the topic of your paragraph, your next step will be to write a topic sentence. The **topic sentence** has specific characteristics.

- It introduces the topic of the paragraph.
- It states the paragraph's controlling idea.
- It is the most general sentence in the paragraph.
- It is followed by other sentences that provide supporting facts and examples.

The **controlling idea** makes a point about the topic and expresses the writer's opinion, attitude, or feeling. You can express different controlling ideas about the same topic. For example, the following topic sentences are about youth offenders, but each sentence makes a different point about the topic.

narrowed topic                      controlling idea
**Youth offenders** should not receive special treatment from the

correctional system.

                           controlling idea
Rehabilitation and education are the best ways for the state to handle
narrowed topic
**youth offenders.**

**ESSAY LINK**

Just as a topic sentence expresses the main point of a paragraph, the thesis statement expresses the main point of an essay. Both have a controlling idea.

### PRACTICE 1

Read each topic sentence. Underline the topic once and the controlling idea twice.

**EXAMPLE:**

<u>Learning to play the guitar</u> <u>requires practice, patience, and perseverance.</u>

1. Music education is essential in public schools.

2. My furnished room has everything a student could need.

3. You can learn to make decisions and think critically with a liberal arts education.

4. Several interesting things happened during the Stanford Prison Experiment.

5. The new youth center has a very impressive design.

6. There should not be a lower legal drinking age in our state.

7. We encountered many problems on our journey to Honduras.

8. Rory was known for his rumpled, unfashionable clothing.

9. IQ tests are not always accurate and valid.

10. The Beatles went through many musical phases.

## Identifying the Topic Sentence

Before you write topic sentences, practice finding them in paragraphs by other writers. To find the topic sentence of a paragraph, follow these steps.

- Read the paragraph carefully.
- Look for a sentence that sums up the paragraph's subject. Professional writers may place the topic sentence anywhere in the paragraph.
- After you have chosen a sentence, see if the other sentences in the paragraph provide evidence that supports that sentence.

If you find one sentence that sums up what the paragraph is about and is supported by other sentences in the paragraph, then you have identified the topic sentence.

### PRACTICE 2

Underline or highlight the topic sentences in paragraphs A, B, and C.

**EXAMPLE:**

<u>Researchers say they have found the remains of a rodent the size of a buffalo in South America.</u> Fossils suggest a 1,545-pound rodent that was a plant eater lived 6 million to 8 million years ago in what was then a lush, swampy forest. Marcelo R. Sanchez-Villagra of the University of Tubingen in Germany described the creature as "a weird guinea pig . . . with a long tail for balancing on its hind legs." The fossils were found in a desert area some 250 miles west of Caracas, Venezuela.

—Lee Krystek, "Strange Science," *Unnatural Museum.com*

A.   The idea of controlling music in society has been around for a long time. About 2,400 years ago, the Greek philosopher Plato said that the types of music people listened to should be controlled by the state. During the Middle Ages and the Renaissance, it was the Church that specified how music should be composed and performed. And in later centuries secular rulers held a virtual monopoly over the music that was allowed in their realm. Often, composers had to submit a work to a committee before it was allowed to be published or performed.

—Jeremy Yudkin, *Understanding Music*

B.   Cosmetic surgery is not like fooling around with a bottle of hair dye or getting a set of fake fingernails. The procedures are invasive, the recovery sometimes painful, and mistakes, while not common, can be difficult or impossible to correct. Breast implants may rupture, noses sink inward, and smiles turn unnaturally tight. People who merely wanted fat vacuumed from their thighs have died, while balding men have found themselves sporting new hair in symmetrical rows like tree farms. Stephen Katz, a sociologist at Trent University in Ontario, Canada, says, "To have plastic surgery, you have to think of your body as an object. It's a kind of social madness."

—Patricia Chisholm, "The Body Builders," *MacLean's*

C.   Imagine a society without laws. People would not know what to expect from one another (an area controlled by the law of contracts), nor would they be able to plan for the future with any degree of certainty (administrative law); they wouldn't feel safe knowing that the more powerful or better armed could take what they wanted from the less powerful (criminal law); and they might not be able to exercise basic rights which would otherwise be available to them as citizens of a free nation (constitutional law).

—Frank Schmalleger, *Criminal Justice Today*

## Writing an Effective Topic Sentence

When you develop your topic sentence, avoid some common errors by asking yourself these three questions.

1. **Is my topic sentence a complete sentence that has a controlling idea?**
   You might state the topic in one word or phrase, but your topic sentence should always reveal a complete thought and have a controlling idea. It should not announce the topic.

|  |  |
|---|---|
| **Incomplete:** | Working in a restaurant. |
|  | (This is a topic but *not* a topic sentence. It does not contain both a subject and a verb, and it does not express a complete thought.) |
| **Announcement:** | I will write about part-time jobs. |
|  | (This announces the topic but says nothing relevant about it. Do not use expressions such as *My topic is . . .* or *I will write about. . . .*) |
| **Topic sentence:** | Part-time jobs help college students build self-esteem. |

**TECHNOLOGY LINK**

If you write your paragraph on a computer, make your topic sentence bold (ctrl B). Then you and your instructor can easily identify it.

2. **Does my topic sentence make a valid and supportable point?**
Your topic sentence should express a valid point that you can support with your evidence. It should not be a vaguely worded statement, and it should not be a highly questionable generalization.

| | |
|---|---|
| **Vague:** | Beauty is becoming more important in our culture. |
| | (Beauty is more important than what?) |
| **Invalid point:** | Beauty is more important than it was in the past. |
| | (Is this really true? Cultures throughout history have been concerned with notions of beauty.) |
| **Topic sentence:** | Fashion magazines do not provide people with enough varied examples of beauty. |

**ESSAY LINK**

If you find that your topic is too broad for a paragraph, you might want to save it so you can try using it for an essay.

3. **Can I support my topic sentence in a single paragraph?**
Your topic sentence should express an idea that you can support in a paragraph. It should not be too broad or too narrow.

| | |
|---|---|
| **Too broad:** | Love is important. |
| | (It would be difficult to write a paragraph about this topic. There are too many things to say.) |
| **Too narrow:** | My girlfriend was born on March 2nd. |
| | (What more is there to say?) |
| **Topic sentence:** | During my first relationship, I learned a lot about being honest. |

 **Write an Interesting Topic Sentence**

Your topic sentence should not express an obvious or well-known fact. Write something that will interest your readers and make them want to continue reading.

**Obvious:** Money is important in our world.
(Everybody knows this.)

**Better:** There are several effective ways to save money.

## PRACTICE 3

Choose the word from the list that best describes the problem with each topic sentence. Correct the problem by revising each sentence.

| Announces | Incomplete | Narrow |
|---|---|---|
| Broad | Invalid | Vague |

**EXAMPLE:**

This paragraph is about television advertisements.

     Problem:      *Announces*

     Revised statement:   *Television advertisements should be banned during children's programming.*

1. How to pack a suitcase.

   Problem: _____

   Revised statement: _____

2. I will write about negative political campaigns.

   Problem: _____

   Revised statement: _____

3. Today's journalists never tell both sides of the story.

   Problem: _____

   Revised statement: _____

4. History teaches us lessons.

   Problem: _____

   Revised statement: _____

5. Deciding to go to college.

   Problem: _____

   Revised statement: _____

6. The subject of this paragraph is school uniforms.

   Problem: _____

   Revised statement: _____

7. Everybody believes in ghosts.

   Problem: _____

   Revised statement: _____

8. The coffee shop walls are painted green.

   Problem: _____

   Revised statement: _____

## The Writer's Desk **Write Topic Sentences**

Narrow each of the topics in this exercise. Then, write a topic sentence that contains a controlling idea. You could look at the Writer's Desk: Narrow the Topic on page 18 for ideas.

**EXAMPLE:** City life

Narrowed topic: Impressions of Las Vegas

Topic sentence: Las Vegas is a vibrant city of extremes.

1. The family

Narrowed topic: _____

Topic sentence: _____

2. Telling lies

Narrowed topic: _____

Topic sentence: _____

3. Travel

Narrowed topic: _____

Topic sentence: _____

4. An issue in the news

Narrowed topic: _____

Topic sentence: _____

5. Jobs

Narrowed topic: _____

Topic sentence: _____

**ESSAY LINK**

When writing an essay, place the thesis statement in the introduction. Then each supporting idea becomes a distinct paragraph with its own topic sentence.

## The Supporting Ideas

Once you have written a clear topic sentence, you can focus on the **supporting details**—the facts and examples that provide the reader with interesting information about the subject matter. There are three steps you can take to determine your paragraph's supporting details.

- Generate supporting ideas.
- Choose the best ideas.
- Organize your ideas.

## Generating Supporting Ideas

You can try an exploring strategy such as brainstorming or freewriting to generate ideas.

### WADE'S SUPPORTING IDEAS

College student Wade Vong narrowed his topic and wrote his topic sentence. Then he listed ideas that could support his topic sentence.

**Las Vegas is a vibrant city of extremes.**

- crowds of tourists
- peaceful suburbs
- beautiful parks and canyons
- superhot summers
- roads lined with palm trees
- lots of beige and pink buildings with clay-tiled roofs
- variety of great entertainment
- Cirque du Soleil has permanent shows
- close to the Grand Canyon
- fast-paced, glitzy tourist strip
- sea of neon lights

*The Writer's Desk* **List Supporting Ideas**

Choose two of your topic sentences from the Writer's Desk on page 24. For each topic sentence, develop a list of supporting ideas.

## Choosing the Best Ideas

An effective paragraph has **unity** when all of its sentences directly relate to and support the topic sentence. Create a unified paragraph by selecting three or four ideas that are most compelling and that clearly support your topic sentence. You may notice that several items in your list are similar; therefore, you can group them together. If some ideas do not support the topic sentence, remove them.

### WADE'S BEST SUPPORTING IDEAS

Wade highlighted three of his most appealing ideas. Then he grouped together related ideas. Finally, he crossed out some ideas that did not relate to his topic sentence.

**Las Vegas is a vibrant city of extremes.**

– crowds of tourists
– peaceful suburbs
– beautiful parks and canyons
– ~~super-hot summers~~
– roads lined with palm trees
– lots of beige and pink buildings with clay-tiled roofs          A
– variety of great entertainment
– Cirque du Soleil has permanent shows          C
– ~~close to the Grand Canyon~~
– fast-paced, glitzy tourist strip
– sea of neon lights          B

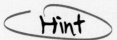  **Identifying the Best Ideas**

There are many ways that you can highlight your best ideas. You can circle the best supporting points and then use arrows to link them with secondary ideas. You can also use highlighter pens or asterisks to identify the best supporting points.

**PRACTICE 4**

College student Sandra Ahumada brainstormed ideas about tipping. Her purpose was to persuade, so she created a topic sentence that expressed her opinion about the issue.

Underline three ideas from her list that you think are most compelling and that most clearly illustrate the point she is making in her topic sentence. Then group together any related ideas under each of the main subheadings. If any ideas do not relate to her topic sentence, remove them.

TOPIC SENTENCE: **Customers should always tip restaurant servers.**

– part of the cost of going to a restaurant
– shows appreciation for the server's work
– servers need tips to have an adequate standard of living
– their salaries below the standard minimum wage
– some customers rude
– servers often don't get benefits such as health care
– you tip hairdressers and taxi drivers
– mistakes aren't always the server's fault
– slow service could be the cook's fault
– sometimes there are not enough servers
– some people in the service industry get good money (cooks, I think)

*The Writer's Desk* **Choose the Best Ideas**

Choose *one* of the two lists of supporting ideas that you prepared for the previous Writer's Desk on page 25. Identify some compelling ideas that clearly illustrate the point you are trying to make. If any ideas are related, you can group them together. Cross out any ideas that are not useful.

## Organizing Your Ideas

To make your ideas easy for your readers to follow, organize your ideas in a logical manner. You can use one of three common organizational methods: (1) time order, (2) emphatic order, or (3) space order.

    **Transitional expressions** help guide the reader from one idea to another. A complete list of transitional expressions appears on pages 43–44 in Chapter 3.

**ESSAY LINK**

In an essay, you can use time, space, or emphatic order to organize your ideas.

### Time Order

When you organize a paragraph using **time order (chronological order),** you arrange the details according to the sequence in which they have occurred. When you narrate a story, explain how to do something, or describe a historical event, you generally use time order.

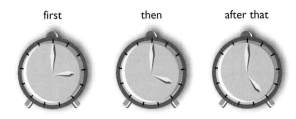

Here are some transitional expressions you can use in time-order paragraphs.

| | | | |
|---|---|---|---|
| after that | first | last | next |
| eventually | in the beginning | meanwhile | suddenly |
| finally | later | months after | then |

The next paragraph is structured using time order.

> One morning, I found out the use of a key. I locked my mother up in the pantry where she was obliged to remain three hours, as the servants were in a detached part of the house. She kept pounding on the door while I sat outside on the porch steps and laughed with glee as I felt the jar of the pounding. This most naughty prank of mine convinced my parents that I must be taught as soon as possible. After my teacher, Miss Sullivan, came to me, I sought an early opportunity

to lock her in her room. I went upstairs with something which my mother made me understand I was to give to Miss Sullivan. No sooner had I given it to her than I slammed the door, locked it, and hid the key under the wardrobe in the hall. I could not be induced to tell where the key was. My father was obliged to get a ladder and take Miss Sullivan out through the window—much to my delight. Months after, I produced the key.

—Helen Keller, *The Story of My Life*

### Emphatic Order

When you organize the supporting details of a paragraph using **emphatic order,** you arrange them in a logical sequence. For example, you can arrange details from least to most important, from least appealing to most appealing, and so on.

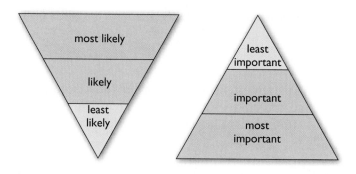

Here are some transitional expressions you can use in emphatic-order paragraphs.

| | | | |
|---|---|---|---|
| above all | especially | moreover | principally |
| clearly | in particular | most importantly | the least important |
| first | last | of course | the most important |

The following paragraph uses emphatic order. The writer presents the conditions from bad ones to worst ones.

The conditions experienced by the eager young volunteers of the Union and Confederate armies included massive, terrifying, and bloody battles, apparently unending, with no sign of victory in sight. First, soldiers suffered from the uncertainty of supply, which left troops, especially in the South, without uniforms, tents, and sometimes even food. They also endured long marches over muddy, rutted roads while carrying packs weighing fifty or sixty pounds. Most importantly, disease was rampant in their dirty, verminous, and unsanitary camps, and hospitals were so dreadful that more men left them dead than alive.

— Adapted from John Mack Faragher et al., *Out of Many: A History of the American People*

When you organize details using emphatic order, use your own values and opinions to determine what is most or least important, upsetting, remarkable, and so on. Another writer might organize the same ideas in a different way.

## Space Order

When you organize ideas using **space order,** you help the reader visualize what you are describing in a specific space. For example, you can describe something or someone from top to bottom or bottom to top, from left to right or right to left, or from far to near or near to far.

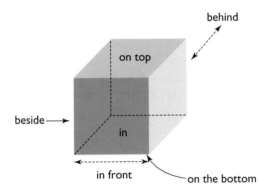

Here are some transitional expressions you can use in space-order paragraphs.

| | | | |
|---|---|---|---|
| above | beneath | nearby | on top |
| behind | closer in | on the bottom | toward |
| below | farther out | on the left | under |

In the next paragraph, the writer describes a location beginning at the beach and ending up at the front of the house.

> Their house was even more elaborate than I expected. It was a cheerful red-and-white Georgian Colonial mansion overlooking the bay. The lawn started at the beach and ran toward the front door for a quarter of a mile, jumping over sundials and brick walks and burning gardens—finally, when it reached the house, drifting up the side in bright vines as though from the momentum of its run. The front was broken by a line of French windows.
>
> —F. Scott Fitzgerald, *The Great Gatsby*

## PRACTICE 5

Read each paragraph and decide what order the writer used: time, space, or emphatic.

A. That night, I lay awake and anxiously listened to the thunder as it continued to get closer and louder. Then I couldn't hear the thunder any more as it was replaced by another sound. I had never heard that sound before but I knew what it had to be. A split second later, I yelled "Tornado!" My wife jumped about two feet. We couldn't even get out of bed. Suddenly, everything was moving, and all we could do was hold on to each other. The roar, the sound of splintering wood and the screeching sound of tearing sheet metal seemed to last forever. In fact, it lasted about 15 seconds. Finally, silence returned like someone flipping a switch.

—Louis M. Tursi, "The Night Crawler"

Order: _____

B. Many factors contribute to racist attitudes. First, there are often higher levels of racist incidents in societies that have historically had very little contact with different ethnic groups. According to writer and political analyst Gwynne Dyer, such isolated societies may feel threatened when there is an influx of immigrants. Moreover, racist attitudes become more prevalent when various ethnic communities do not intermingle. If different cultural communities do not work and study together, stereotypes about other groups become entrenched. Most importantly, high levels of poverty contribute to racist reactions; immigrants become easy and available scapegoats when there is competition for limited jobs.

—Eliot Mandel, student

Order: _____

C. The bomb had demolished a group of houses two hundred meters up the street. A black plume of smoke hung in the sky, and below it a cloud of plaster dust in which a crowd was already forming around the ruin. There was a little pile of plaster lying on the pavement ahead of him, and in the middle of it he could see a bright red streak. When he got up to it, he saw that it was a human hand severed at the wrist.

—George Orwell, *1984*

Order: _____

## PRACTICE 6

Read the following topic sentences. Decide what type of order you can use to develop the paragraph details. Choose space, time, or emphatic order. (There may be more than one correct organizational method.)

**EXAMPLE:**

Learning to play the guitar requires practice, patience, and perseverance.                     *Emphatic*

1. Music education is essential in public schools. _____

2. My furnished room has everything a student could need.                                      _____

3.  You can learn to make decisions and think critically with a liberal arts education.  _____

4.  Several interesting things happened during the Stanford Prison Experiment.  _____

5.  The new youth center has a very impressive design.  _____

6.  There should not be a lower legal drinking age in our state.  _____

7.  We encountered many problems on our journey to Honduras.  _____

8.  Rory was known for his rumpled, unfashionable clothing.  _____

9.  IQ tests are not always accurate and valid.  _____

10.  The Beatles went through many musical phases.  _____

# The Paragraph Plan

A **plan,** or **outline,** of a paragraph is a map showing the paragraph's main and supporting ideas. To make a plan, write your topic sentence, and then list supporting points and details. Remember to use emphatic, time, or space order to organize the supporting points. In a more formal outline, you can use letters and numbers to indicate primary and secondary ideas.

### WADE'S PARAGRAPH PLAN

Wade completed his paragraph plan. He narrowed his topic, wrote a topic sentence, and thought of several supporting details. Here is his paragraph plan.

**ESSAY LINK**

Make a plan when you write an essay. In essay plans, each supporting idea becomes a separate paragraph.

TOPIC SENTENCE:   **Las Vegas is a vibrant city of extremes.**

Support 1:   Peaceful suburbs integrate the desert landscape.
Details:   —roads lined with palm trees
—beige and pink buildings with clay-tiled roofs
—beautiful parks and canyons

Support 2:   The tourist strip is fast-paced and glitzy.
Details:   —roving crowds of tourists
—sea of neon lights
—massive replicas of pyramids, Eiffel Tower

Support 3:   There is a huge variety of entertainment.
Details:   —Cirque du Soleil has permanent shows
—well-known singers such as Celine Dion perform there
—hypnotists and magicians in clubs
—gambling for every taste and budget

 **Adding Specific Details**

When you prepare your paragraph plan, ask yourself if you have enough supporting details. If not, then you could add details to make your points stronger. For example, when Wade first brainstormed a list of supporting details (page 25) he thought of only one detail to support his point about the great variety of entertainment in Las Vegas. In his paragraph plan, however, he decided to add a few more details (Céline Dion, hypnotists, magicians, gambling) to make that point stronger and more complete.

## *The Writer's Desk* **Write a Paragraph Plan**

Look at the topic sentence and the organized list of supporting ideas that you created for the previous Writer's Desk exercises. Now, in the space provided, make a paragraph plan. Remember to include details for each supporting idea.

Topic
sentence: _____

_____

Support 1: _____

Details: _____

_____

Support 2: _____

Details: _____

_____

Support 3: _____

Details: _____

_____

## Writing the Concluding Sentence

A stand-alone paragraph may have a **concluding sentence** that brings it to a satisfactory close. There are several ways to write a concluding sentence.

- Restate the topic sentence in a new, refreshing way.
- Make an interesting final observation.
- End with a prediction, suggestion, or quotation.

 **Problems with Concluding Sentences**

When you write your concluding sentence, do not introduce a contradictory idea or change the focus of the paragraph. For example, in Wade's paragraph about Las Vegas, he should not end with a statement that questions or contradicts his main point.

**Weak:**    Las Vegas can be a bit boring.

(This concluding sentence undermines the main point, which is that Las Vegas is a vibrant city of extremes.)

**Better:**    If you would like to visit a truly unique city, go to Las Vegas.

(This suggestion brings the paragraph to a satisfactory close.)

## PRACTICE 7

The topic sentences in paragraphs A and B are underlined. For each paragraph, circle the letter of the most effective concluding sentence, and then explain why the other choice is not as effective.

**EXAMPLE:**

Picasso painted many different types of people that he saw in the Paris neighborhood of Montmartre. He painted musicians, prostitutes, street vendors, circus performers, and fellow artists, as well as his many lovers. During his blue period, he was drawn to emaciated figures; impoverished mothers and hungry children populated his art.

a. Picasso painted many different types of people.

(b.) The human body was ultimately the most important and repeated image in his paintings and sculptures.

Why is the other choice not as effective?

*Sentence "a" just repeats the topic sentence.*

A. Our state should insist that day-care centers provide more flexible hours for families. Today, in many families, both parents work outside the home. These parents do not necessarily work from nine to five. For example, nurses and factory employees work in shifts. For such parents, flexible day care is very important. Also, many parents who are in the service and retail industry work on weekends. For these parents, it is important to have adequate child-care facilities during their work hours.

a. The current opening hours of most day-care centers do not meet the needs of a great number of families.

b. However, maybe day-care owners do not want to open on nights and weekends.

Why is the other choice not as effective?

_____

B. <u>College students should find part-time jobs that require them to exercise different muscles.</u> If a business student spends hours sitting in front of a computer screen, then he should try to find a job that requires physical activity. If an engineering student has to do advanced calculus, then maybe her part-time job should allow her to rest her brain. Students who do a lot of solitary study could try to find jobs that allow them to interact socially.

a. Some college students should not take part-time jobs because they need to concentrate on their studies.

b. Humans need to do a variety of activities to be mentally and physically strong, so college students should keep that in mind when they look for work.

Why is the other choice not as effective?

_____

## PRACTICE 8

Read the next paragraph by college student Veena Thomas. Then answer the questions that follow.

After completely immersing myself in college life for nine months, it was easy to forget the existence of normal civilization, so returning home for the summer was an awakening. First, I had my own room, but no roommates for company and conversation. My house was amazingly clean. There were no dust bunnies under the furniture, and there was no dirty ring in the bathtub. The food at dinner was delicious, and it was free! It was always nutritious and beautifully prepared.

1. What is the topic of this paragraph?

_____

2. Underline the topic sentence.

3. List the supporting details.

_____

_____

_____

4. Write two possible concluding sentences for this paragraph.

a. _____

_____

b. _____

_____

# The First Draft

After making a paragraph plan, you are ready to write your first draft, which is a very important step in the writing process. Your first draft includes your topic sentence, some supporting details, and a concluding sentence.

As you write your first draft, you might find it difficult sometimes to say what you mean. If you are having trouble, underline that section or put a check mark beside it so that you can come back to revise it later. If possible, put your first draft aside for a few hours before rereading it. Then, when you revise your paragraph, you will read it with a fresh perspective. The next chapter contains information about revising a paragraph.

### WADE'S FIRST DRAFT

Here is Wade Vong's first draft. You may notice that his paragraph has errors. He will correct these when he gets to the revising and editing stage of the process.

> **Las Vegas is a vibrant city of extremes.** Peaceful suburbs integrate the desert landscape. Neighborhoods have pink and beige buildings with clay-tiled roofs, many yards contain various species of cactus. White roads are lined with palm trees. There are beautifull parks and canyons. Other parts of the city are extremely fast-paced and glitzy. On the Las Vegas Strip, neon lights illuminate the night sky. Crowds of tourists gaze at massive replicas of the pyramids, the Statue of liberty, and the Eiffel Tower. The strip is also vibrant because of the great entertainment available, including gambling for every taste and budget. The city attract world-class entertainment. Such as Celine Dion. The Cirque du Soleil has permanent shows. Even small clubs have magicians and hypnotists. If you would like to visit a truly unique city, go to Las Vegas.

## The Writer's Desk  Write Your First Draft

In the previous Writer's Desk on page 32, you made a paragraph plan. Now use the plan's information to type or write your first draft paragraph.

## REFLECT ON IT

Think about what you have learned in this chapter. If you do not know an answer, review that topic.

1.  What is a topic sentence? _____

    _____

2.  What is time order? _____

    _____

3.  What is emphatic order? _____

    _____

4.  What is space order? _____

    _____

Are the following sentences true or false? Circle the best answer.

5.  A paragraph has more than one main idea.              True    False

6.  A paragraph's details support its topic sentence.        True    False

 **The Writer's Room**  **Topics to Develop**

## Writing Activity 1

In the Writer's Room in Chapter 1, "Exploring," you used various strategies to find ideas about the following topics. Select one of the topics and write a paragraph. Remember to follow the writing process.

### General Topics

1. a childhood memory
2. anger
3. rules
4. cosmetic surgery

### College and Work-Related Topics

5. a comfortable place
6. study or work habits
7. gossip
8. cell phones

## Writing Activity 2

Choose a topic that you feel passionate about and write a paragraph. Your topic could be an activity (painting, basketball) or an interest (music, politics). Your topic sentence should make a point about the topic.

### DEVELOPING CHECKLIST

As you develop your paragraph, ask yourself the following questions.

Have I narrowed my topic?

Does my topic sentence make a valid and supportable point about the topic?

Is my topic sentence interesting?

Does my paragraph focus on one main idea?

Do the details support the topic sentence?

Do the supporting details follow a logical order?

Does my paragraph end in a satisfactory way?

B. Orville and Wilbur Wright had an unlikely dream, but they turned it into reality. When the brothers first tried to make a plane fly, they were unsuccessful. In fact, in 1901, a frustrated Wilbur Wright said that humans wouldn't fly for a thousand years. However, just two years later, on December 17, 1903, Wilbur and Orville Wright flew a plane for 105 feet. The brothers were overjoyed; their hard work and planning had finally paid off. Since that time, air travel has changed a lot. Many different types of planes exist today. Jets fly across our skies and can go from London to New York in a few hours. Eventually the Wright brothers produced nineteen types of aircraft. By sticking with an idea and persevering, the Wright brothers made their dream a reality.

## Revise for Adequate Support

**ESSAY LINK**

When revising your essay, ensure that you have adequately supported the thesis statement. Also ensure that each body paragraph has sufficient supporting details.

A paragraph has **adequate support** when there are enough details and examples to make it strong, convincing, and interesting. The following paragraph attempts to persuade, but it does not have any specific details that make a strong point.

In European films, the star can be wrinkled or overweight. **Unfortunately, American filmmakers have not figured out that people like to see reflections of themselves on screen.** To get a job, American movie actors must be in perfect shape and have perfect bodies. It is often hard to believe that the beautiful actor is really the waiter or car mechanic that is pictured on screen. The problem is especially acute when the star is older. You can be sure that he or she has had a lot of surgery to look as young as possible. Ordinary audience members have trouble identifying with surgically enhanced actors. Perhaps one day American producers will use regular-looking people in their films.

### PRACTICE 2

When the preceding paragraph about film stars is expanded with specific details and examples, the paragraph becomes more convincing. Try adding details on the lines provided. You can do this alone or with a partner.

In European films, the star can be wrinkled or overweight. Unfortunately, American filmmakers have not figured out that people like to see reflections of themselves on screen. To get a job, American movie actors must be in perfect shape and have perfect bodies. For example, _____ and _____ are incredibly good-looking. It is often hard to believe that the beautiful actor is really the waiter or car mechanic that is pictured on screen. In the movie titled _____, the actor _____ looks too perfect to be a _____.

The problem is especially acute when the star is older. You can be sure that he or she has had a lot of surgery to look as young as possible. For instance, _____ looks much younger than the actor's real age. Ordinary audience members have trouble identifying with surgically enhanced actors. Perhaps one day American producers will use regular-looking people in their films.

## Avoiding Circular Reasoning

**Circular reasoning** means that a paragraph restates its main point in various ways but does not provide supporting details. The main idea goes in circles and never progresses. Avoid using circular reasoning by providing a clear, concise topic sentence and by supporting the topic sentence with facts, examples, statistics, or anecdotes.

### CELIA'S PARAGRAPH

Celia Raines, a student, wrote the following paragraph about a popular proverb. In the paragraph, she repeats her main point over and over and does not provide any evidence to support her topic sentence.

> **Circular**  Those who make the most noise usually get what they want. People sometimes shout and make a fuss and then others listen to them. Those who are quiet get ignored and their opinions do not get heard. It is important for people to speak up and express their needs. This attitude is expressed in the proverb "The squeaky wheel gets the grease."

In the second version of this paragraph, Celia added a specific example (an anecdote) that helped illustrate her main point.

> **Not Circular**  Those who make the most noise usually get what they want. Those who are quiet get ignored, and their opinions do not get heard. For example, two years ago, the local government started a passenger train service that helped local commuters get into the city. Many citizens loved commuting by train, but those who live near the train tracks complained about the noise. They made petitions, wrote to newspapers, and lobbied the local government to cancel the train service. Those people were so loud and persistent that they got their wish and the train service was canceled. The silent majority disagreed with that lobby group, but as the proverb says, "The squeaky wheel gets the grease."

## PRACTICE 3

Paragraphs A and B use circular reasoning. There is no specific evidence to support the topic sentence. List supporting examples for each paragraph. With numbers, indicate where you would place the supporting examples.

**EXAMPLE:**

American teenagers go through several rites of passage. These rites of passage help the teenager navigate the transition from childhood to adulthood. (1) Some rites of passage are shared with the community. (2) These rites are an important part of every youth's life.

Examples:    (1) the first date and the first kiss

the first job

(2) the high school prom

A.  Police officers have an important function in our society. They provide many useful and necessary services in the community. If there were no police officers, there would be anarchy in the streets. Law-enforcement officers deserve our respect and appreciation.

Examples: _____

_____

_____

_____

_____

_____

_____

B.  When you move out of your family home and live on your own, you should plan your budget carefully. There are many things that you will have to pay for, and a lot of items will be expensive. You will need to pay for services. Even small household items add up. It is expensive to live on your own.

Examples: _____

_____

_____

_____

_____

_____

_____

# Revise for Coherence

When you drive along a highway and you suddenly hit a pothole, it is an uncomfortable experience. Readers experience similar discomfort if they encounter potholes in a piece of writing. Make your writing as smooth as possible by ensuring that it has **coherence:** the sentences should flow smoothly and logically.

## Transitional Expressions

**Transitional expressions** are linking words or phrases, and they ensure that ideas are connected smoothly. Here are some common transitional expressions.

**ESSAY LINK**

To create coherence in an essay, you can place transitional expressions at the beginning of each body paragraph.

| Function | Transitional Word or Expression | |
|---|---|---|
| **Addition** | again | in addition |
| | also | in fact |
| | besides | last |
| | finally | moreover |
| | first (second, third) | next |
| | for one thing | then |
| | furthermore | |
| **Concession of a point** | certainly | of course |
| | even so | no doubt |
| | indeed | to be sure |
| **Comparison and contrast** | as well | likewise |
| | equally | nevertheless |
| | even so | on the contrary |
| | however | on the other hand |
| | in contrast | similarly |
| | instead | |
| **Effect or result** | accordingly | otherwise |
| | as a result | then |
| | consequently | therefore |
| | hence | thus |
| **Example** | for example | in particular |
| | for instance | namely |
| | in other words | specifically to illustrate |
| **Emphasis** | above all | least of all |
| | clearly | most important |
| | first | most of all |
| | especially | of course |
| | in fact | particularly |
| | in particular | principally |
| | indeed | |
| **Reason or purpose** | for this purpose | the most important reason |
| | for this reason | |
| **Space** | above | near |
| | behind | nearby |
| | below | on one side / on the other side |
| | beneath | on the bottom |
| | beside | on the left/right |
| | beyond | on top                    *(continued)* |

| Function | Transitional Word or Expression | |
|---|---|---|
| **Space** | closer in | outside |
| | farther out | to the north/east/south/west |
| | inside | under |
| **Summary or conclusion** | in conclusion | therefore |
| | in other words | thus |
| | in short | to conclude |
| | generally | to summarize |
| | on the whole | ultimately |
| **Time** | after that | later |
| | at that time | meanwhile |
| | at the moment | months after |
| | currently | now |
| | earlier | one day |
| | eventually | presently |
| | first (second, etc.) | so far |
| | gradually | subsequently |
| | immediately | suddenly |
| | in the beginning | then |
| | in the future | these days |
| | in the past | |

 **Use Transitional Expressions with Complete Sentences**

When you add a transitional expression to a sentence, ensure that your sentence is complete. Your sentence must have a subject and a verb, and it must express a complete thought.

**Incomplete:** For example, the rules posted on the wall.

**Complete:** For example, the rules <u>were</u> posted on the wall.

### PRACTICE 4

The next paragraph contains eight transitional expressions that appear at the beginning of sentences. Underline each expression, and then, in the chart, indicate its purpose. The first one has been done for you.

For those who love eating out, a new type of dining experience is rearing its ugly head. <u>Indeed</u>, service with a sneer is popping up in Canada and the United States. For instance, in the New York City teahouse Tea and Sympathy, customers must follow a rigid list of rules. Those who plan to wait for friends are sharply told to leave. Moreover, patrons who manage to get a table are kicked out as soon as they finish their tea. Similarly, in Vancouver, the Elbow Room Café posts rules on the wall, including one that asks customers to get their own coffee and water. Also, the owner and staff members ridicule customers. Even so, clients keep coming back, comparing the experience to going to a show. The bad service trend has always been there. However, people in previous decades would have left such eateries without leaving a tip. These days, customers line up to be abused.

| Transitional Expression | Function |
|---|---|
| 1.  Indeed | Emphasis |
| _____ | _____ |
| _____ | _____ |
| _____ | _____ |
| _____ | _____ |
| _____ | _____ |
| _____ | _____ |
| _____ | _____ |

## PRACTICE 5

Add appropriate transitional expressions to the following paragraph. Choose from the following list, and use each transitional word once. There may be more than one correct answer for each blank.

| | | |
|---|---|---|
| furthermore | as a result | in fact |
| first | on the whole | for example |

The most interesting college course I have ever had was Introductory Psychology 101. _____, I found the course material very interesting because the textbook contained true case studies. _____, my instructor was the most stimulating teacher I have ever had. He used humor to engage the students' attention. _____, I enjoyed going to class. _____, my instructor had found a way to make the horrible experience of taking exams interesting. His exams were so original that I looked forward to test periods. _____, he devised tests and exams in the form of mysteries to solve. The solution to each question lay in the problem that we had studied in each chapter of our textbook. _____, Introductory Psychology 101 was the most appealing course I have ever taken.

# Revise for Style

When you revise for sentence **style,** you ensure that your paragraph has concise and appropriate language and sentence variety. You can ask yourself the following questions.

**ESSAY LINK**

You should also revise your essays for style, ensuring that sentences are varied and parallel. Also, ensure that your language is exact.

- Have I used a **variety of sentence patterns?** (To practice using sentence variety, see Chapter 19.)
- Have I used **exact language?** (To learn about slang, wordiness, and overused expressions, see Chapter 31.)
- Are my sentences **parallel in structure?** (To practice revising for parallel structure, see Chapter 21.)

### WADE'S REVISION

On page 35 in Chapter 2, you read the first draft of student Wade Vong's paragraph about Las Vegas. Look at his revisions for unity, support, coherence, and style.

Transition ➤

Detail ➤

Las Vegas is a vibrant city of extremes. ~~Peaceful~~ *First, peaceful* suburbs integrate the desert landscape. ~~Neighborhoods~~ *Some neighborhoods stunning* have pink and beige buildings with clay-tiled roofs, many yards contain various species of cactus. White roads ~~are~~ lined with palm trees.

Combined sentences ➤

Transition ➤

Detail ➤

~~There are~~ *lead to* beautifull parks and canyons. ~~Other~~ *In contrast, other* parts of the city are extremely fast-paced and glitzy. On the Las Vegas Strip, *for instance,* neon lights illuminate the night sky. Crowds *jostling* of tourists gaze at massive replicas of the pyramids, the Statue of liberty, and the Eiffel Tower. The strip is also vibrant because of the great entertainment available, including gambling for every taste and

Transition ➤

Combined sentences ➤

budget. ~~The~~ *In addition, the* city attract world-class entertainment. Such as Céline Dion. The Cirque du Soleil has permanent shows. ~~Even~~ *, and even* small clubs have magicians and hypnotists. If you would like to visit a truly unique city, go to Las Vegas.

---

 **Adding Strong Support**

When you revise, look at the strength of your supporting details. Ask yourself the following questions.

- Are my supporting details interesting, and do they grab the reader's attention? Should I use more vivid words?

- Is my concluding sentence appealing? Could I end the paragraph in a more interesting way?

---

## PRACTICE 6

In Chapters 1 and 2, you saw examples of Sandra Ahumada's prewriting and planning. Now look at the first draft of Sandra's paragraph, and revise it for unity, support, and coherence. Also, ask yourself what you could do to enhance her writing style.

> Customers should always tip restaurant servers. Servers need tips to live. Their salary is very low. They depend on tips to pay for food, housing, and other necessities. They do not get benefits such as health care. If you do not like the service, remember that mistakes are not always the server's fault. Poor service could be the cook's fault. Sometimes there are not enough servers. I work as a server in a restaurant. I know how hard it is when customers leave bad tips. Always tip your restaurant server.

# Edit for Errors

When you **edit,** you reread your writing and make sure that it is free of errors. You focus on the language, and you look for mistakes in grammar, punctuation, mechanics, and spelling.

There is an editing guide in the rear of this book. It contains some common error codes that your teacher may use. It also provides you with a list of things to check for when you proofread your text.

## Editing Tips

The following tips will help you proofread your work more effectively.

- Put your writing aside for a day or two before you do the editing. Sometimes, when you have been working closely with a text, you might not see the errors.
- Begin your proofreading at any stage of the writing process. For example, if you are not sure of the spelling of a word while writing the first draft, you could either highlight the word for later verification or immediately look up the word in the dictionary.
- Keep a list of your common errors in a separate grammar log. When you finish a writing assignment, consult your error list, and make sure that you have not repeated any of those errors. After each assignment has been corrected, you could add new errors to your list. For more information about grammar and spelling logs, see Appendix 7.

### WADE'S EDITED PARAGRAPH

Wade Vong edited his paragraph about Las Vegas. He corrected errors in spelling, capitalization, punctuation, and grammar.

> **Las Vegas is a vibrant city of extremes.** First, peaceful suburbs integrate the stunning desert landscape. Some neighborhoods have pink and beige buildings with clay-tiled roofs, _and_ many yards contain various species of ~~cactus~~ _cacti_. White roads lined with palm

_beautiful_
trees lead to ~~beautifull~~ parks and canyons. In contrast, other parts of the city are extremely fast-paced and glitzy. On the Las Vegas Strip, for instance, neon lights illuminate the night sky. Crowds of jostling tourists gaze at massive replicas of the pyramids, the Statue
_Liberty_
of ~~liberty~~, and the Eiffel Tower. The strip is also vibrant because of the great entertainment available, including gambling for every
_attracts_
taste and budget. In addition, the city ~~attract~~ world-class
_such_
entertainment.~~.~~ ~~Such~~ as Céline Dion. The Cirque du Soleil has permanent shows, and even small clubs have magicians and hypnotists. If you would like to visit a truly unique city, go to Las Vegas.

## The Writer's Desk **Revise and Edit**

Choose a paragraph you wrote for Chapter 2, or choose one that you have written for another assignment. Carefully revise and edit the paragraph. You can refer to the Revising and Editing Checklist at the end of this chapter.

## Peer Feedback

After you write a paragraph or essay, it is useful to get peer feedback. Ask another person such as a friend, family member, or fellow student to read your work and give you comments and suggestions on its strengths and weaknesses.

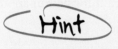 **Offer Constructive Criticism**

When you peer-edit someone else's writing, try to make your comments useful. Phrase your comments in a positive way. Look at these examples.

| **Instead of saying . . .** | **You could say . . .** |
|---|---|
| Your sentences are boring. | Maybe you could combine some sentences. |
| Your supporting ideas are weak. | You could add more details here. |

You can use the following peer feedback form to evaluate written work.

# Peer Feedback Form

Written by: _____  Feedback by: _____

Date: _____

1. What is the main point of the written work?

_____

2. What details effectively support the topic sentence?

_____

3. What, if anything, is unclear or unnecessary?

_____

4. Give some suggestions about how the work could be improved.

_____

5. What is an interesting or unique feature of this written work?

_____

_____

# Write the Final Draft

When you have finished making revisions on the first draft of your paragraph, write the final draft. Include all of the changes that you have made during the revision and editing phases. Before you hand in your final draft, proofread it one last time to ensure that you have caught any errors.

## The Writer's Desk **Write Your Final Draft**

You have developed, revised, and edited your paragraph. Now write the final draft. Before you offer it to readers, proofread it one last time to ensure that you have found all of your errors.

 Spelling, Grammar, and Vocabulary Logs

• **Keep a spelling and grammar log.** You probably repeat, over and over, the same types of grammar and spelling errors. You will find it very useful to record your repeated grammar mistakes in a spelling and grammar log. You can refer to your list of spelling and grammar mistakes when you revise and edit your writing.

• **Keep a vocabulary log.** Expanding your vocabulary will be of enormous benefit to you as a writer. In a vocabulary log, you can make a list of unfamiliar words and their definitions.

## REFLECT ON IT

Think about what you have learned in this chapter. If you do not know an answer, review that topic.

1. What are four things that you should look for when revising?

   _____     _____

   _____     _____

2. Circle the best answer(s). A paragraph is unified if

   a. there are no irrelevant supporting details.

   b. there are many facts and statistics.

   c. all details support the topic sentence.

3. Circle the best answer: Transitional words are _____ that help ideas flow in a logical manner.

   a. links          b. sentences          c. verbs

4. The Editing Handbook in Part IV includes information about grammar, spelling, and punctuation errors. In what chapter would you find information about the following topics? Look in the table of contents to find the chapter number.

   a. Capitalization            _____

   b. Subject-verb agreement    _____

   c. Faulty parallel structure _____

   d. Commas                    _____

   e. Commonly confused words   _____

 The Writer's Room **Paragraph Topics**

## Writing Activity 1

Choose a paragraph that you have written for work or another course. Revise and edit that paragraph, and then write a final draft.

# Writing Activity 2

Choose any of the following topics, or choose your own topic. Then write a paragraph. Remember to follow the writing process.

**General Topics**

1. interesting things about yourself
2. how to write a paragraph
3. heroes in the media
4. the meaning of the quotation at the beginning of this chapter
5. bad service

**College and Work-Related Topics**

6. something you learned in a college course or on campus
7. an unusual work experience
8. reasons to turn down a job
9. telemarketing
10. an interesting job

## ✔ REVISING AND EDITING CHECKLIST

When you revise and edit, ask yourself the following questions. (For a more detailed editing checklist, refer to the inside back cover of this book.)

**Unity**

☐ Is my paragraph unified under a single topic?

☐ Does each sentence relate to the topic sentence?

**Support**

☐ Does my paragraph have an adequate number of supporting details?

**Coherence**

☐ Is my paragraph logically organized?

☐ Do I use transitional words or expressions to help the paragraph flow smoothly?

**Style**

☐ Do I use a variety of sentence styles?

☐ Is my vocabulary concise?

☐ Are my sentences parallel in structure?

**Editing**

☐ Do my sentences contain correct grammar, spelling, punctuation, and mechanics?

## TEXT:

**Page 9**: Carol R. Ember and Melvin Ember, *Cultural Anthropology*, 10th ed., © 2002. Reprinted by permission of Pearson Education, Inc., Upper Saddle River, NJ; **p. 8**: Reprinted by permission of Jake Sibley; **p. 20**: Reprinted by permission of The Museum of Unnatural Mystery; **p. 21**: Jeremy Yudkin, *Understanding Music*, 3rd ed., © 2002. Reprinted by permission of Pearson Education, Inc., Upper Saddle River, NJ; **p. 21**: Reprinted by permission of *Maclean's Magazine*; **p. 21**: Frank Schmalleger, *Criminal Justice Today: An Introductory Text for the 21st Century*, 6th ed., © 2001. Reprinted by permission of Pearson Education, Inc., Upper Saddle River, NJ; **p. 27**: From Helen Keller, *The Story of My Life*. W.W. Norton & Company, Inc. © 2003. Reprinted with permission; **p. 28**: John M. Faragher, Susan H. Armitage, Mari Jo Buhle, Daniel Czitrom, *Out of Many*, Combined Brief 4th ed., © 2004. Reprinted by permission of Pearson Education, Inc., Upper Saddle River, NJ; **p. 29**: Reprinted by permission of Louis Tursi; **p. 56**: Reprinted by permission of Dinesh D'Souza; **p. 68**: Jeremy Yudkin, *Understanding Music*, 3rd ed., © 2002. Reprinted by permission of Pearson Education, Inc., Upper Saddle River, NJ; **p. 90**: Reprinted by permission of Joel Ceausu; **p. 102**: Reprinted with permission of Paul Sabourin; **p. 115**: Frank Schmalleger, *Criminal Justice Today: An Introductory Text for the 21st Century*, 6th ed., © 2001. Reprinted by permission of Pearson Education, Inc., Upper Saddle River, NJ; **p. 128**: ©2004 by Dawn Rosenberg McKay (http://careerplanning.about.com). Used with permission of About, Inc., which can be found on the Web at http://www.about.com. All rights reserved; **p. 129**: Reprinted by permission of Dorothy Nixon; **p. 130**: Reprinted by permission of Ellen M. Zavian, Sports Attorney/Professor; **p. 156**: Copyright © 2003 by the New York Times Co. Reprinted by permission; **p. 168**: Reprinted by permission of Veena Thomas; **p. 183**: Linda L. Lindsey and Stephen Beach, *Essentials of Sociology*, 1st ed., © 2003. Reprinted by permission of Pearson Education, Inc., Upper Saddle River, NJ; **pp. 183 & 184**: Robert Paul Wolff, *About Philosophy*, 8th ed., © 2000. Reprinted by permission of Pearson Education, Inc., Upper Saddle River, NJ; **p. 184**: Albert M. Craig, William A. Graham, Donald Kagan, Steven Ozment, and Frank M. Turner, *Heritage of World Civilizations*, Combined Brief 1st ed., © 2002. Reprinted by permission of Pearson Education, Inc., Upper Saddle River, NJ; **p. 186**: Reprinted by permission of Dorothy Nixon; **p. 195**: Reprinted by permission of Stephen Lautens; **p. 200**: Reprinted by permission of Jeff Kemp; **p. 205**: Reprinted by permission of Rahul Goswami; **p. 210**: Reprinted by permission of Jake Sibley; **p. 215**: Reprinted with permission of Diego Pelaez; **p. 241**: Copyright © 2003 by the New York Times Co. Reprinted by permission; **p. 242**: Martin Seligman, "The American Way to Blame," July 1998, *APA Monitor*, page 2. Copyright © 1998 by the American Psycho-logical Association. Adapted with permission; **p. 244**: Carol R. Ember and Melvin Ember, *Cultural Anthropology*, 10th ed., © 2002. Reprinted by permission of Pearson Education, Inc., Upper Saddle River, NJ; **p. 246**: Daniel R. Brower, *The World in the Twentieth Century: From Empires to Nations*, 5th ed., © 2002. Reprinted by permission of Pearson Education, Inc., Upper Saddle River, NJ; **p. 293**: Rita Dove, *Time Magazine*, Special Issue: "Time 100: Heroes and Icons of the Twentieth Century," June 14, 1999, Vol. 153, No. 23; **p. 530**: From Maya Angelou, *Wouldn't Take Nothing for My Journey Now*. Copyright © 1993 by Maya Angelou. Used by permission of Random House; **p. 533**: Reprinted by permission of *Nation's Restaurant News*; **p. 536**: From *Natural Health*, Jan.-Feb. 2003. © 2003 Weider Publi-cations, LLC. Reprinted with permission; **p. 538**: Reprinted by permission of Deborah Mead; **p. 541**: Reprinted by permission of Josh Freed; **p. 545**: Text as submitted from Judy Scheindlin and Josh Getlin, *Don't Pee on My Leg and Tell Me It's Raining*. Copyright © 1996 by Judy Scheindlin and Josh Getlin. Reprinted by permission of HarperCollins Publishers, Inc.; **p. 548**: Copyright © 2004 by the New York Times Co. Reprinted by permission; **p. 552**: Scott Bekker, "Nothing But Net," August 30, 2000, http://www.entmag.com. Vallejo Communications; **p. 554**: David A. Locher, *Collective Behavior*, 1st ed., © 2002. Reprinted by permission of Pearson Education, Inc., Upper Saddle River, NJ; **p. 557**: Reprinted by permission of Raul Reyes; **p. 560**: Courtesy of Bebe Moore Campbell; **p. 562**: Reprinted by permission of MacNeil-Lehrer Pro-ductions; **p. 565**: Richard Rodriguez, "It's CLASS, Stupid." Copyright © 1997 by Richard Rodriguez. Originally appeared in *Salon* (Nov. 1997). Reprinted by permission of Geeorges Bordchardt, Inc., for the author; **p. 572**: Mitch Albom, "Body Over Mind?" *The Detroit Free Press*, April 11, 1995. Reprinted by permission of TMS Reprints; **p. 575**: H.D., "Dying to Be Bigger, *Seventeen*, December 1991; **p. 580**: Copyright © 1991 by Globalflair Ltd.; **p. 583**: Leslie Marmon Silko, *Yellow Woman and a Beauty of the Spirit*. Reprinted with permission of Simon & Schuster Adult Publishing Group. Copyright © 1996 by Leslie Marmon Silko; **p. 586**: Richard Selzer, *Moral Lessons: Notes on the Art of Surgery*. Copyright © 1974 by Richard Selzer. Reprinted by permission of Georges Borchardt, Inc., for the author; **p. 589**: Reprinted by permission of cbc.ca

## PHOTOS:

**Page 15**: Violence Policy Center; **p. 16**: Frank Whitney/Getty Images, Inc.-Image Bank; **p. 37**: Catherine Wessel/Corbis/Bettmann; **p. 63**: Jerzy Kolacz/Getty Images, Inc.-Image Bank; **p. 64**: Spots on Spots; **p. 75**: Phil Degginger/Picturesque Stock Photo; **p. 86**: Photomondo/Getty Images, Inc.-Taxi; **p. 99**: Milton Greene/Picture Post/IPC Magazines/Getty Images; **p. 111**: Tim Jonke/Getty Images, Inc.-Image Bank; **p. 124**: Corbis Digital Stock; **p. 138**: left, Corbis/Bettmann; right, AP Wide World Photos; **p. 151**: Tobi Corney/Getty Images, Inc.-Stone Allstock; **p. 153**: Comstock Images/Getty Images, Inc.-Comstock Images Royalty Free; **p. 166**: Corbis Digital Stock; **p. 169**: Dallas and John Heaton/The Stock Connection; **p. 266**: Christoph Wilhelm/Getty Images, Inc.-Taxi; **p. 330**: © AFP/Corbiss; **p. 345**: Paul Gilligan/Getty Images, Inc.-Artville LLC; **p. 358**: Art Montes de OCA/Getty Images, Inc.-Taxi; **p. 389**: Michael Newman/PhotoEdit; **p. 405**: The Bridgeman Art Library International Ltd.; other photos from photos.com

# Index